Garden
HINTS & TIPS

Garden
HINTS & TIPS

Karen Farrington

igloo

This book was first published in 2004 in Great Britain
by Igloo Books Ltd., Henson Way, Telford Way Industrial Estate,
Kettering, Northants NN16 8PX
info@igloo-books.com

This book was created for Igloo Books
by Amazon Publishing Ltd., 7 Old Lodge Place, Twickenham,
Middlesex, TW1 1QR

Author Karen Farrington
Editor Mary Davies
Designer Maggie Aldred

ISBN 1-84561-018-0
Printed and bound in China

Foreword

As gardening becomes more popular, there is an ever greater
demand for horticultural know-how and advice. This rise in
popularity has been matched by an increased environmental
awareness, which in turn has led to a greater emphasis on the use
of natural techniques over harsher chemical alternatives wherever
possible. This book provides a wide range of green hints and tips
suitable for the budding novice and weathered gardener alike.
These have been collated from a wide range of sources, mostly,
of course, from my own experience and from fellow gardeners
and garden designers, but also from magazines, books, manuals
and the internet, to provide the reader with a broad range of
the best techniques. Please note, it is important that due caution
is taken when using chemicals, products and techniques outlined
in this book, and that their success cannot be guaranteed.
All treatments should be tested prior to application, in
an inconspicuous place, and please read and follow all
information on product labels with care.

Contents

Plants and Flowers

Flowers and plants can brighten almost any location in and around the home, from colourful borders and creative containers to indoor plants, window boxes and hanging baskets. Try these helpful hints to ensure blooming success whatever the weather.

Garden Know-how

Gardening is a subtle combination of visual flair, scientific know-how, intuition and not a small helping of hard labour. Here are some general points to remember whatever your interest.

If you are to make informed choices about how your garden should look, you need to understand the changing face of the plot throughout the different seasons. If you have moved house, don't embark on a major garden re-fit for a year, so you can check what, when and where plants appear. Make notes and take photos (don't forget to date them) to help clarify your ideas.

Why not use a digital camera to record your gardening successes – and failures – through the year? Then you can keep a permanent record of your garden calendar on computer, together with notes to help you hit the highs – and avoid the pitfalls – in future growing seasons.

For a garden to succeed, it is important that the location and conditions are suitable for the plants and flowers in it. That means taking note of the weather conditions, the soil type and the direction that your garden faces. Soil testing kits are readily available from garden centres and are especially important if you're about to invest in a costly shrub or time-consuming crop.

In general terms, add lime to acid soil to make it more neutral and add peat moss, sawdust or pine needles to introduce acidity.

Buy plants only from outlets which obviously have the facilities to care for them. Trays of plants may look inviting on a garage forecourt but can you be sure they've been properly protected on cold nights? And are supermarket plants tended properly – getting the light and water they require – while they remain unsold on the premises?

Plants on sale in garden centres have usually been kept under glass. If they are destined to live outside, don't forget to 'harden' them off. That means giving them some protection in the open at first so they can gradually get used to more exposed conditions. Otherwise your purchase is likely to keel over quickly.

Native plants are more likely to thrive and survive than those imported from overseas.

Flower Borders

A successful flower border bursts with a riot of colour and vitality that fuels the imagination and leaves a lasting impression upon many budding gardeners. Achieving this effect in your own garden, however, is not always such a walk in the park. So here are some simple tricks and trade secrets for achieving chocolate box charm.

Don't ditch hyacinth bulbs from Christmas presentation displays. They'll never achieve the same glory in the pot again, but you can plant them into the border as an outside bulb. Remove the dead flowering heads, keep the compost from drying and plant out in April. They are happiest in the shelter of a tree or shrub.

Daffodil abuse is widespread – gardeners become irritated with the floppy foliage once the flower is gone and cut it back too early. Try, however, to resist the temptation to cut, tie or knot the leaves for about six weeks, when the leaves naturally fade, as they are still making food for the bulb to use in next year's growing period.

Plant a scattering of nigella or candytuft around daffodils
so their later spring growth will mask the daff's dying leaves.

It's vital to warm the soil before planting out new additions to
the border. You could use plastic sheeting or a glass cloche,
but canny gardeners simply chop up empty two-litre lemonade bottle
to do the same job. Just press the cut end firmly into the soil and
leave the bottle bottom or top pointing upwards. These mini-cloches
work well in pots too, and you can control ventilation by adding
or taking away the bottle top.

Grow extra plants to barter with friends and neighbours.
You'll get a wide variety at a fraction of the cost of those on sale
at a garden centre and you might pick up invaluable tips on
cultivation too.

There are internet websites devoted to plant swapping.
Use your favourite search engine and type in the name of the plant
you are looking for followed by the word 'swapping'.

Aquilegias or columbines are easy to maintain. They sprout
and spread energetically and are immensely decorative. But don't
hesitate to pop May or June-flowering plants in front of them to
hide tatty foliage when the blooms fade.

Grow sweet pea seeds in empty toilet-roll holders to encourage
a long, strong root system. The cardboard will not disintegrate
until the plant is ready to be moved to its final position.
Rolls of newspaper also make cheap, biodegradable pots.

It's best to plant in groups and in odd numbers. Three, five or seven together always look more natural and less regimented than two, four or six.

If you're planning a new border, mark out its proposed dimensions with sand and 'shade' it in so you can get a clear view of how it will look when complete.

Use boulders to flank a flight of steps. They provide the perfect antidote to stark margins and an ideal environment for alpines and low-growing rock plants that like their heads in sun but their roots in shade.

Always tear – rather than cut – suckers off roses as near to the base as possible. Cutting will cause the suckers to multiply.

Buy 'past their best' plants at garden centres when they
are on offer for knock-down prices. A bit of tender loving
care will invariably bring the casualty back to life.

Use the flower border as an extension to the vegetable plot by
planting decorative and delicious greens. A glance through the
seed racks will offer numerous choices. Chard, in particular, deserves
special mention, as it has a wonderfully pleasing form, comes in stalks
of striking colour and is versatile in the kitchen.

Don't dump fading pansies and violas. Cut them back hard
and new shoots should develop in a few weeks. This can prolong the
life of these cheery plants for at least a season.

Stylish garden borders often feature sculpture. However, these delightful focal points can be expensive to buy, so why not take a trip to the beach in search of your very own natural, individual and free ornament in the form of an interesting piece of driftwood, fashioned by the tides into an intriguing shape? Your one-off ornament will be a talking point and, if it loses its appeal, can be burnt on the bonfire.

It's relatively easy to chop down a tree but far more demanding to dig out the stump. So turn it into an unusual feature by digging in lashings of garden compost to enrich the soil and then planting frothy ferns at its base. If, in time, your stump is swamped by greenery, add in a few more logs of varying size from the wood shed to create your own 'stumpery'.

Indian summers can be difficult for camellias as they need water to form flower buds for the following spring. Make sure they get a soaking during dry autumns to prevent excessive bud drop.

Dry summer flowers to enjoy the blooms all winter long.
You need to plant suitable varieties in spring, including lavender,
Nigella, chives, *Monarda*, teasels, sea holly, golden rod and feverfew.
Pick in a dry spell after the dew has cleared but before midday,
choosing only perfect blooms. Hang upside down in small bunches
away from direct sunlight to preserve as much colour as possible.
If you want to collect seeds, tie a muslin bag around the bunch
during the drying process.

Rose cuttings are no more difficult to take than other
woody cuttings. In autumn, select several of this year's healthy
stems that measure about 25cm (10in). Cut below a shoot at the base
of each stem and above a shoot at the top, to eliminate the
growing tip. Remove all the leaves but two on each cutting,
plunge it into hormone rooting-powder, and then place with several
others in a large pot of gritty compost or a protected garden
trench. Water well and one or more of the cuttings should be
ready to plant out by the following summer.

Pick flowers in the morning, using a sharp knife rather than scissors or clippers, and place them in clean, tepid water out of direct sunlight. If you are arranging a mixed bunch which includes daffodils, don't recut the daffodil stems when you put them in the vase as they secrete a compound which can harm other flowers.

Hanging Baskets and Containers

Not everyone has a vast expanse of green outside the back door, but most of us have space for a few pots or baskets which, strategically placed, can make a potentially barren space somewhere leafy and special.

Don't skimp. A large, generously overflowing container has a much greater impact than a dozen small ones containing the same or a greater number of plants.

It's tempting to spread all the plants you have between the available containers. But it is worth keeping some back so that you can replace fatalities without additional cost.

Choose plants that match the proportions of the pot. Tiny alpines do not look at home in huge pots.

Prolong the life of a cracked garden pot by
circling its rim with strong wire, using pliers to twist
the ends firmly together.

Terracotta pots look sensational on a sun-baked patio
but they are always thirsty. Before planting up a terracotta or
clay container, soak it in water so it won't immediately
leach all moisture from the new compost. And consider
sinking terracotta pots into the border during hot summers
to prevent unnecessary water evaporation.

It is surprising how little moisture from a summer shower
penetrates a planted pot so don't rely on rain to water containers.
Make a habit of checking the container compost each day, no matter
what the weather, to be sure it's neither too dry or too wet.

Plants need to be watered only when the soil is dry to the touch, so don't water by the clock. Always water in the morning or the evening so as little as possible evaporates.

Try putting a couple of used teabags in the bottom of pots and containers before you plant them up to help to retain moisture.

Beware of those pots and hanging baskets where drought has shrunk the compost in the container, as water will simply rush right past the roots and out of the bottom, soaking your feet rather than the soil. One solution is to buy compost with a wetting agent, which helps break the natural surface tension of the water and thus makes it more easily absorbable by the compost.

A simple, cheap and effective method of effectively watering thirsty baskets is to incorporate a 2 to 4-inch empty pot in the top of the finished design. Add the water to this pot, and it will act as a reservoir to hold the water whilst it soaks into the basket.

Don't forget to feed hanging baskets. Regular watering is essential but the water running out of the bottom takes with it valuable nutrients which must be replaced if flowers and foliage are to flourish.

Containers can look wonderful but it takes a lot of effort to keep them in top condition. You can achieve the same effect by knocking the bottoms out of old or damaged containers and placing them on a bed of soil. The plants will root down into the ground and need much less watering in the summer months.

During heavy rainfall, prop containers carefully on their sides
so the soil doesn't become waterlogged and the crowns of the plants
don't suffer rain damage.

You can protect fragile plants from unseasonal frost by insulating
the container with bubblewrap and covering the foliage with
horticultural fleece or some old net curtain.

Add flair to a modern arrangement and enhance the colours
of the plants by using a coloured mulch, such as coloured gravel
or recyled glass chippings.

For shady spots, consider an all-green container display.
The key to success is using as many different types of foliage as
your budget will allow. Architectural palms, frothy ferns, grasses,
ivy, herbs and even conifers, grouped in different pots, can blend to
create a magnificently verdant effect.

Variegated leaves may be out of fashion with garden designers,
but they can help to lift a dull spot. Try the green and red *Pelargonium*
'Mrs Quilter' or varieties of colourful *Solenostemon*.

If you plant a container with scented flowers, try and position
it near a door or window, where it won't be knocked over, so you get
the benefit of its aroma indoors too.

Plant herbs in containers near the kitchen window so you can easily
reach out and pick the required herb whilst cooking.

For an unusual outside wall decoration, use a willow obelisk
as a wall-mounted plant basket. Line the upturned obelisk to
the halfway mark with moss, and then a discreet sheet of black plastic,
before filling with compost. Push the roots of your chosen plants
through the willow struts of the top half so that stems and flowers
will provide a layer of flora and foliage outside the obelisk. Top up
with moss and compost and plant up. Choose bright yellows, oranges
and reds so the obelisk becomes a flaming medieval torch.

Why not create a living house-number outside the front door?
Using a suitably sized pot, plant small echeverias to form the required
figure and fill the background with contrasting yellow
Sagina subulata 'Aurea'. Apart from an occasional trim,
it should be maintenance-free.

Houseplants

The lush foliage of a rampant houseplant brings the freshness of the great outdoors to even the smallest urban flat, while homes without greenery can feel like a domestic desert. Use these simple techniques for healthier, happier houseplants all year round.

More houseplants are killed by overwatering than neglect so resist the inclination to keep soil moist. When the soil appears dry, stand the pot in water for about half an hour, then discard any remaining water. A plant's need for water depends on its position and room conditions, so don't be afraid to use your own judgement.

Did you know that plants such as the spider plant, ivy, bamboo palm, fig tree and mother-in-law's tongue are all said to improve air quality? NASA scientists claim houseplants could help purify the air inside a space shuttle, so they are likely to be good for the home too.

If you mist or spray your houseplants on a regular basis, avoid using water from the tap, especially if it's known to be 'hard', as it may lead to white marks on the leaves. The alternatives are rainwater or boiled (and cooled!) tap water.

Uproot a snowdrop or two from your garden and wash off the soil clinging to its stem. Place the bulb and its root in shallow water and enjoy a long-lasting display of springtime splendour.

For some cats, the lure of a large houseplant as an indoor toilet is too great to resist. Make it altogether less attractive by keeping pierced lemons or oranges – or just their aromatic peel – close to the target plant and sprinkling the soil with black pepper. Cats find citrus and pepper a turn-off and would rather brave the great outdoors whatever the weather.

Sap-sucking insects, such as aphids and whitefly, often move in on
houseplants and are happy to kill the host if they have to. Try washing
an affected plant with soapy water, applied with a brush or a spray or,
if the leaves are large, wiped clean. Small plants can also be dunked
in a bucket. Rinse off any soapy water with clean tepid water.
Resort to an insecticide only if that fails – no one wants
to spray chemicals around the home.

Never place a houseplant on top of the television. It's usually
too warm and often too far from adequate light.

Houseplants enjoy being outside in the summer for
some refreshing sunshine and rainwater. But don't shift
them into the garden too quickly as they suffer
from night chills in a cold snap.

When you've run out of favours with the neighbours and no one
will water your plants while you're on holiday, try soaking the pots,
draining them and putting them into clear plastic bags.
Use sticks to fan out the plastic and make some air holes for
succulents. Secure the bags and leave the plants in their
mini-greenhouses until your return.

You can create a delightful gift by planting up an indoor garden.
Three-quarters fill a waterproof bowl with crocks and soil.
Then place a tall plant at the back, two bushy flowering plants in the
centre and a trailing plant in the front. It's best to split the plants once
the flowers have dropped and preserve them singly, otherwise
the roots become tangled.

On cold nights, take precautions with houseplants kept on the
windowsill by slipping a sheet or two of paper between glass and
leaves or, better still, moving the plants to a more protected spot.

Houseplants suffer a double assault in winter – dark days and central heating both put the plant under stress. To combat these factors, place a humidifier, if you have one, near the plants so they can enjoy its invigorating air flow. Or stand the plant pot in a tray of dampened pebbles so water evaporates upwards onto the leaves. Even when the soil is damp the leaves may be parched, so spray occasionally to freshen them up.

Production Zones

Nothing beats organic, home-grown fruit, vegetables and herbs, so whether you have a veg plot, an allotment, a greenhouse or simply a windowbox, these trusty tips will help you achieve the unmistakeable taste of green-fingered success.

Vegetable Gardens

**The pleasure of picking produce from the garden
and serving it up just a few hours later can make hours of
back-breaking toil worthwhile. Certainly the flavour of home
produce is far superior to anything available on a supermarket
shelf. Here are some ways to take the labour pains
out of the veggie patch.**

To produce the best possible crop of seed potatoes, start 'chitting'
from late January. In other words, stand them blunt end uppermost in
trays (without soil) somewhere they can enjoy plenty of light. They'll
be ready for planting out when the shoots are about 2.5 cm (1in) long.

For a swift and rewarding remedy to a bare garden, try sowing
different types of lettuce. This humble salad leaf now comes
in numerous shapes, sizes and colours and will transform even flower
borders at speed. Although lettuce plants can be thinned, they don't
like being transplanted, so leave them where you start them off.

Don't plant seeds directly into the soil outside until the temperature is a steady 15°C (or 60°F). Hasty sowing puts the crop at risk.

Seeing a row of seedlings standing tall is always a thrill and makes the task of thinning out all the more heartbreaking. However, the most successful vegetables come from plants that had room to spread their roots and grow, which is why thinning – the unacceptable face of gardening – must take place.

Plant sweetcorn in squares of four or nine in a block. The system increases the plants' chances of pollination. If your flower border is big enough, pop a square in there too, as sweetcorn is ornamental as well as tasty. The plants need to be 35cm (14ins) apart so there's ample space to plant something in between. (Eat the cobs as soon as possible after harvesting as the natural sugars begin turning into starch the minute they are plucked.)

Fig trees grow well in milder climates, but be sure to contain the roots. A small bed no more than 75cm (30in) wide, or a large pot, are ideal.

Brighten your salad bowl this summer with the petals of edible flowers. Some of the most popular are nasturtiums, bergamot, borage, heartsease and pot marigolds. Most large seed companies offer packets of these easy-growers for home germination. Make sure you check before you eat: many plants and their flowers are poisonous, and you should never eat flowers which have been sprayed, including those from a florist.

Tie peppers to canes for support, and mist regularly to deter red spider mites. Once the plants start to swell, add a potassium-rich feed to the watering regime.

You can transform a plain wall into a vertical veggie patch with a little DIY. Cover the wall with a wire mesh on timber supports to provide framework. Then attach pots and small troughs securely with wire, making allowance for plant growth. Use polysterene chips to provide drainage and reduce pot weight, and choose miniature varieties of container vegetables such as cherry tomatoes, aubergines, chillies, lettuce, basil and rocket. Keep everything well watered. South-facing walls will do best.

If you spot blight on a potato crop you need to act fast. At first sight of the tell-tale black and withered marks on the foliage, cut off the affected leaves and burn them. The tubers below ground won't swell any further but it will prevent them from spoiling. Copper-based fungicides might save the rest of the crop but again rapid action is essential.

Grow your own new potatoes for the Christmas table by potting up 'second-cropping' seed potatoes, which have been treated to achieve swift growth, in August. In mild areas, the crop might succeed in open soil, but growing times will be quicker still if pots are brought into a greenhouse in bad weather.

Don't hang about when harvesting sweet potatoes. They are best pulled when the tubers are small and immature because even a slight frost causes damage. Have your garden fork at the ready at the first sign of wilting vines. Sweet potatoes can be stored for short periods in cool, dark places.

Seeds from home-grown tomatoes can last for ten years if collected and stored properly. Harvest when the tomatoes are at their ripest, then cut them in half and squeeze the pulp into a bucket. Leave the bucket in a warm place to ferment for three to four days. This process kills many diseases and breaks down the gel around the raw seed, which prevents germination. Add water, strain through a sieve, and rinse the seeds thoroughly before leaving on a plate for a couple of weeks, making sure you stir them frequently so they dry completely. Store in labelled, air-tight polythene bags in a cool, dark place.

Carrots don't need rich soil, as too much goodness encourages split stalks and root hairs. One traditional way of preparing soil for carrots is to spread fireplace ashes where they will be planted in the spring.

Give soil a nitrogen boost after harvesting beans by leaving plant roots in the soil after cutting off the stems to remove the dying foliage. The roots break down during the winter months to provide a rich source of nitrogen.

Don't trash leeks or onions that have gone to seed before snipping off the ornate flower heads. These can be dried inside the house and added to winter flower arrangements.

When harvesting spring and summer varieties of cabbage, cut with a sharp knife at ground level, and then score the top of the stump with a cross, to encourage a second crop.

Fill the 'hungry gap' in your vegetable garden with kale and sprouting broccoli. Both are ready in the early spring when there are very few homegrown veggies about.

Vegetable gardens need feeding for best results, but double-digging is history. Instead, spread manure over the empty bed in autumn and let nature do the hard work. By spring the frost will have crumbled it, the rain washed the goodness into the ground, and the worms will have tugged the remains below the surface. All that's left for you to do then is a swift turnover and a rake before planting up.

Different vegetables give – and take – various elements
from the ground. Employ a simple plan of crop rotation to keep
the soil from becoming pest-ridden or going stale. There are
many options but the simplest is to divide the plot into quarters
and in year 1 plant potatoes, celery and leeks in one section,
brassicas (greens) in the second, peas, beans and onions
in the third, and other root crops in the fourth. Rotate the
crops around the quarters in a four-yearly cycle.

Herbs

**Herbs are plants that do more than tickle
the taste buds. Planted separately in formal
arrangements or among flowers and vegetables,
they are attractive, aromatic and wonderfully versatile
additions to the garden, which have the added benefit
of being easy to grow.**

Turn a raised bed into a scented seat by carpeting the
top with herbs – thyme works very well. You'll have to check for
bees before you sit though.

Try to site a herb garden close to the kitchen and barbeque to save
yourself getting footsore in the summer months.

Don't plant fennel near dill or coriander. They will
cross-pollinate and produce indeterminate, unproductive offspring.

Traditionally, the time to sow parsley is Good Friday, but
most spring sowing should be successful. Don't give up on parsley
seeds — they can take up to six weeks to germinate in a
greenhouse or two months outdoors. And remember, parsley
does better in full light.

Unless you want a garden full of mint, confine its root
to a pot. There are numerous varieties and they look stunning
grouped in terracotta pots. Other herbs that benefit from
being pot-bound are bergamot, oregano and lemon balm.

Pop a bay leaf into the flour bin in the kitchen to keep away
the weevil that thrives in flour stores.

When you run out of bubble bath in the summer, toss a handful of mint into the water. Not only is its scent delicious but it is said to soothe and strengthen the nerves.

Drying herbs for use at a later date will bring a touch of sunshine and a reminder of summer to the dullest winter day. Gather on a dry summer day, binding them together in small bunches. Hang upside down in a warm, dry, airy place, out of direct sunshine which will dull their colour, for several days until they are dry to the touch. Spread the leaves singly on a sheet of cooking foil and heat in a low oven for a short spell to complete the drying process. Store in airtight glass jars. Remember: dried herbs have a stronger flavour than fresh, so use sparingly.

Keep a potted basil plant on the windowsill to deter flies.
They hate its pungent aroma.

Strip the foliage from rosemary twigs to create
home-grown kebab skewers. The remaining hint of flavour
means they are especially good with lamb.

Greenhouses

Crops grow more quickly under glass than in the great outdoors, so households with a greenhouse can enjoy an early harvest. It's also a place of warmth and tranquility for much of the year, providing a cosy retreat for a break from outdoor gardening

Don't overwater seedlings in a greenhouse as they soon rot in the warm and wet environment. Also, avoid getting water on the stem of a seedling at the point where it meets the soil.

Many plants reared in a greenhouse won't get the benefit of visiting insects, so use a cotton bud or a paint brush to transfer pollen from one flower to the next. Repeat the process the following day.

When you run out of individual cells to rear seedlings, fill a seed
tray with compost and cover it with 1.3cm ($^1/_2$in) mesh wire.
Plant a seed through each hole in the mesh for even spacing and then
remove the mesh before growth begins.

Seedlings reared in greenhouses tend to get 'leggy' because
they have life so easy. Pass your hand or a piece of paper gently
across the seedling tops a dozen times a day to imitate a light breeze
and encourage them to stockiness.

When potting on seedlings, line the drainage hole with a
leaf so compost isn't washed away. The leaf will soon rot, leaving a
seedling with a strong root system that won't be disturbed
when you transplant.

To water thirsty plants – such as melons and cucumbers – in grow bags, submerge an old plastic drinking cup with a hole in the bottom next to each plant to the depth of the roots. Then simply pour water into the cup and it's delivered where it's most needed. And don't forget to cut drainage holes in grow bags to prevent them becoming waterlogged.

Fit wire mesh to the lower sections of your greenhouse glass, on the outside. You'll have some protection if you slip and fall against the glass, and it acts as a football shield too!

Store any unused seed after sowing in a tin where it can remain cool and dry, and packets should last for three seasons. That's a real money-saver if you're planting just a little at a time.

If your dibber looks too big and clumsy to pot on
really fine seedlings in the greenhouse, use a cocktail stick instead.
Or transplant a small group of seedlings together.

Allotments

Allotments can provide a sanctuary from the modern world, a haven from the hubbub and an antidote to stress. They offer an opportunity to flex your creative and physical muscles – producing top quality, healthy, organic food whilst gently exercising the body in a calm, outdoors setting. Here are a few pointers to getting, and keeping, an allotment the painless way.

A full plot measures about 10 rods (about 9m x 28m or 30ft x 90ft). If this sounds too much like hard work, inquire about half plots. All local authorities have a duty to provide allotments and most accommodate requests for smaller sites, although you may have to join a waiting list.

The terms of the lease could curtail your activities on the plot so study it carefully before you commit. There may be restrictions on building a greenhouse, for example, or planting fruit trees.

Check that the site of the allotment has a ready water supply.
No amount of tender loving care will make up for a lack of aqua.

Talk to allotment holders about their experiences on the site.
Night intruders – either human or animals such
as deer – may warrant the swift installation of defences.

Choose slow-growing, low-maintenance vegetables if you are going to be hard pressed to visit routinely a couple of times a week. Potatoes, onions, squashes and some beans do well even if pressures of work keep you away from the allotment for a week or two.

Standing on soil makes it compact and so less fertile. Stand on a plank when you are working among the veggies – it will distribute your weight evenly and avoid damaging the soil structure.

Save yourself unnecessary labour by covering unused areas with carpet or polythene sheeting. It may not look pretty but it's a great way to keep down the weeds.

Other allotment holders may be amenable to reciprocal holiday-care arrangements and to crop swaps when you have a glut.

Garden Maintenance

Gardens are fragile eco-systems and require watchful tending.

To maintain the natural balance, the right sort of pesticides

and fertilisers have to be correctly applied and pests of all types

need to be carefully controlled in as natural a way as possible.

Weed Control

Have you wimped out on weeding? Do you despair that, given the same warm, wet conditions, weeds shoot up whilst your cultivated plants slow down? You are not alone. Weeds are the single biggest factor in people giving up on their gardens. Luckily, there are many effective and easy ways to deal, and live, with these green invaders.

It sounds self-righteous but here goes, 'A little weeding every day helps to keep a big job at bay.' If you hoe little and often, it stops weeds before they get started and eliminates a potentially back-breaking chore. There's that other well-worn maxim too, 'Many hands make light work.' Bring your partner and any available children to the task.

Weed your garden in damp conditions. It's the only way the blighters give up easily, and it's a tall order to weed a patch of bone-dry soil and stay cheerful.

Invest in the correct tools for the job and weeding will become
far less of a chore. Daisy grubbers – a sturdy prong with a shaped
end – which will lift pesky plants from the lawn, roots and all,
are extremely useful, as are hoes and rakes, which can be used
to expose, uproot and kill young weeds.

Most weeds germinate in the top 5cm (2in) of soil, and
seeds that are buried any deeper rarely push through to the
surface. So avoid digging deep as that's likely to give life to
long-buried weeds.

The dandelion is a formidable adversary. Pour salt over the remaining
root once you've dug up as much of the plant as you can.

A cheap alternative to proprietary chemical weed killers is distilled vinegar. Once drenched in this environmentally friendly acid, a plant is swiftly pickled. For particularly tough customers, try heating the vinegar before applying it. A concentrated dose of salt will also sometimes beat the offender into submission.

Kill weeds with kindness – by introducing a programme of soil improvement. This works best against unwanted plants that prefer an acidic soil. Lavish quantities of compost and mulch will create the alkaline environment they hate and make it far easier to uproot the weeds.

Mulching deprives weed seeds of light and so kills them off. Although mulch is available at garden centres, why not use grass clippings, straw, newspaper, sawdust, black plastic, cardboard or even carpet? The more unsightly options can be disguised with a covering of chippings. Be generous.

Mulch should be at least 10cm (4in) deep.
Compost needs to be generating a heat of over
60°C (140°F) to kill off intruder seeds, so make sure the heap is
functioning properly before adding weeds. It's safer to leave them to
rot in a bucket of water and then add that to the heap.

Don't add animal manure to the garden as it's likely
to be filled with weed seeds. Add it to the compost heap,
where they'll fry.

In the veggie patch make good use of green manure – a crop
that is grown simply to be ploughed back into the soil as fertiliser –
outside the growing season. It smothers the ground so weeds are
suppressed, brings nitrogen to the soil and can be dug in during
the spring to add more organic matter.

Twenty-first-century gardening is being shaped by a new tolerance of nature, and when it comes to weeds that means 'live-and-let-live'. The effort spent eradicating every weed might be better ploughed into cultivating a splendid bloom that detracts the eye from low-growing garden invaders. Some weeds are pretty, some weeds are helpful and some just happen.

Pest and Disease Control

There's nothing quite so demoralizing as seeing a healthy crop or beautiful bloom destroyed overnight. But don't throw in the trowel. There are remedies that keep the bugs at bay. Arm yourself with some effective tactics in the war of the garden pests.

Regular weeding helps to control garden bugs. Groundsel and sow-thistle, for example, harbour leaf miner, whose young burrow inside leaves leaving a white trail in their wake. Weed cover also provides the dark, moist environment that snails and slugs love to breed in, so clearance can pay off twice over.

Nematodes, a type of worm, are an expensive yet often effective biological control for slugs but they don't work well against adult snails, so be sure it is slugs causing plant damage rather than their shell-lugging cousins before investing in some.

One of the best ways to get rid of snails is to attract a thrush to your garden and provide it with a flat stone on which to smash their shells. Another cheap option is to lay an empty grapefruit skin on the soil to attract local slugs and snails. You'll be able to remove a small colony in one fell swoop. Shallow bowls or tin cans containing milk or beer are also irresistible to molluscs, who tend to topple in and drown.

Crushed egg shells, applied liberally around stems, will defend tender plants from snails at little cost without putting pets and wild birds at risk. This also helps to build up calcium levels in the soil. (For slug control, substitute eggshells with soot or sharp gravel.)

Construct 'steps' to allow frogs and toads easy access to a pond. Frogs, and particularly toads, are mighty predators of the hated slug.

To stop ants nesting in pot bottoms, cover the drainage hole
with part of a pair of old tights. If ants – and slugs – are
still a problem, pop the whole pot into the toe of a leg of
tights to halt their progress.

Ants can be a garden pest, not least because they herd aphids and
protect them. But, like most insects, they do have their benefits too:
if your soil is heavy, their activities can help to aerate it
and improve drainage, and they also help to distribute
the seeds of some plants.

Cut out small circles of cardboard or carpet underlay, snip
to the centre and lay them like a collar around the stems of brassicas.
This will halt the progress of the female cabbage-root fly as
she tries to lay her eggs beneath the plant. Any eggs deposited
on the cut-out circle will perish.

Use fine netting to cover cabbages, sprouts and so forth in the summer months. It will discourage determined cabbage white butterflies, whose grubs can strip a patch within days.

Are your broadbeans blighted with blackfly? Try planting English marigolds alongside the crop. The orange flowers are a beacon for hoverfly, which like nothing better than feasting on the blackfly. French marigolds, on the other hand, will help to ward off white fly when planted next to tomatoes.

To avoid disease and deter pests, ensure a row of carrots is fully covered by good-quality fleece from the moment they are put in the ground. Bury the ends in the soil so access remains impossible. If the sight of billowing fleece drives you mad, try planting coriander, onions or garlic to deter the damaging carrot-root fly.

Used coffee grouts laid down between rows of carrots will
help to prevent carrot rust.

Rhubarb leaves make an effective organic pest spray which is
harmless to bees and biodegrades very quickly in the soil, unlike
chemical sprays. Simply boil about 500g (1lb) rhubarb leaves in a litre
of water for 20 minutes using an old pan no longer used for cooking –
the leaves are poisonous and will both stain and contaminate the pot.
Leave to cool, strain and then dissolve 25g (1oz) soap flakes into
the solution. Pour into a spray bottle and label clearly, then keep
safely away from pets and children.

To deter most trunk-climbing caterpillars and insects, place a piece
of sticky tape around the trunk, about 50cm (20in) from the base.
Alternatively, try planting rue around the base of trees attacked by
aphids. Rue is said to transfer its bitter taste to the tree sap,
making it unappetizing to bugs.

Ladybirds eat aphids by the score and planting wormwood
(*Artemisia absinthium*) will attract the red and black insects into the
border for some early-season feasting.

Kill mealy bugs – small, white, cottony creatures – on houseplants
by touching them with a cotton wool bud dipped in alcohol.

When choosing seeds, look for varieties that have been bred
for pest resistance. 'Symphony' strawberries, for example, not only
grow in all soil types and produce an abundant crop with an excellent
flavour, but they also have some resistance to the vine weevil, while
'Lady Balfour' and 'Sante' potatoes escape unscathed from
the double eel worm.

Spray mildew with a 9:1 solution of water and semi-skimmed
milk – it's cheap and organic.

There's anecdotal evidence that copper wire threaded through a tomato plant stem in the autumn will arrest the progress of blight.

Avoid composting rose and tomato leaves. They can spread disease to next year's crops.

Coat the stems of chrysanthemums with petroleum jelly to halt the march of earwigs.

Cats can be a pain in the garden, but fortunately there are many ways to deter them. Try sprinkling a few drops of citronella or eucalyptus oil on some old tea bags and place them around the perimeter of your garden. To keep them out of your flowerbeds, scatter a few mothballs or coal-tar soap shavings among the plants.

Garden Safety

A day in the garden promises to be a relaxing, rewarding affair. Yet the great outdoors hides a host of hazards, and as many as one in five accidents occurs in the garden. Take note of the warnings below and make your backyard a safer place.

Whatever the weather, choose sturdy boots to keep your toes intact when mowing and digging.

Full-length trousers are a wise choice, and use tough gloves for heavy-duty chores like bramble-clearing. The thin variety don't offer enough protection from thorns.

Use rubber gloves when handling garden chemicals. Measure out only as much as you need and keep the rest safely in its original packaging so you have the instructions next time you use it.

Store chemicals in a locked, frost-free cupboard out of
reach of children and pets.

Don't maintain an uncomfortable position for hours during weeding
or you will suffer severe aches and pains the following morning.

You can make your own kneelers from old baby-changing mats
or roll mats used for camping. The latter are especially good as they
are long and you won't have to move them so often.

You should always make sure you use plenty of sunscreen,
wear a hat and drink a lot of water when gardening in the
glare of the sun. This helps to prevent dehydration and the nasty
headache which can accompany it, as well as protecting against
sunburn and sunstroke.

Assess any garden task before embarking on it. Can you manage it alone? Put the job off until help is at hand if necessary, or you may risk the long term health and strength of your back and other vital joints. Always bend from the knees when lifting heavy weights.

Decorative cane tops designed to prevent sticks from poking into eyes are available from garden centres – at a price. Economize by making use of corks, ping-pong balls, potatoes and even the teats from feeding bottles. Just about any soft stopper will do.

Plant sap dries hard on secateur blades if it's not wiped away immediately, and this inhibits the action. If you've neglected the blades in this way, bring them back to form by applying white spirit with a scouring pad. And don't forget to oil their moving parts several times during the season.

Slate paths turn into skating rinks after spells of ice and frost,
and even a short, sharp downpour can create a skidpan. Replace
with alternative materials along main routes and use the
slates for ornamental purposes.

Scatter bonfire ashes on frozen paths and driveways to reduce
the risk of slipping while on foot or driving.

Even a puddle poses a potential threat to toddlers.
Children have been known to drown in as little as 3cm (1in) of water.
If you have youngsters, or some are visiting, ensure containers are
emptied after rain showers and buckets are upturned.

Garden clutter has a habit of lurking in corners and, given half a chance, will multiply like bacteria. It's hard on the eye and can be a hazard. Tedious as it seems, good gardeners clean up as they go along. That way they avoid unnecessary trips and slip-ups.

Learn to identify poisonous plants or you could end up cultivating a killer. The biggest threat is poison ivy, which is luckily still rare in Britain. Many domestic plants, however, are toxic or an irritant. Beware of foxgloves, laburnum, heracleum (or hogweed), castor oil plants, yew, oleander, deadly nightshade, autumn crocuses, lily of the valley and aconitum. Fortunately most poisonous plants taste unpleasant, but always be wary of berries that look succulent, which could have a disastrous effect on your stomach and nervous system.

Garden tools are rich pickings for thieves. One insurance company calculates that gardeners suffer an average loss of £135 every time their shed is burgled. But there are precautions you can take. Each item can be marked with your postcode, for example. This not only deters crooks but also ensures stolen property is returned, if recovered. Contact your local police station to see what services it offers. Assistance will almost certainly be free of charge.

Around the Garden

Most gardens are made up of distinct areas, each requiring

different care and attention. These can range from man-made

structures such as patios and paths to lawns and natural

areas where wildlife can take refuge.

Patios and Paths

Even the best-tended plants need a framework to display them at their finest and provide safe access. This is where patios and paths play their part, as cleverly designed hard landscaping can alter the perspective of a plot, dividing it into distinct zones or making it appear larger than it actually is.

A patio doesn't have to be attached to the side of the house. It is far more important that it is sited in a sunny and perhaps secluded spot.

Mistakes in planning paths and patios are costly and time-consuming to correct, so gather as much advice as you can before laying a slab. Use cardboard squares cut to scale to plan and model a path or patio before you buy any paving. That way you'll avoid either spending too much money or finding you have too few slabs.

A patio is only as good as the foundation it's built upon and that should be 10–15cm (4–6in) deep. Skimp on the base and the patio will quickly deteriorate.

Tables and chairs that constantly wobble are a real pain. To achieve a level finish, choose brick, paving or even terracotta tiling rather than cobbles or gravel.

Reclaimed brick is a popular choice for patios. But beware of bricks with a high salt content because they will crumble quickly. Many bricks are fine for the task but the wrong variety would mean disaster, so inquire before you buy.

Gone are the days when it was wise to choose large tiles
rather than go to the effort of laying small ones. Diminutive
slabs are now available on a roll, with each secured to its
neighbour on a wire mesh. Be aware, however, that the rolls are
heavy and make patio projects a two-person operation.

Avoid using white, or predominately white, stones to
cover large areas of patio or pathway. On sunny days the reflected
light can be painfully bright.

Wall-to-wall paving can look monotonous so incorporate a
few gaps at the planning stage. You can fill them with cobbles, gravel
or some low-growing plants – thyme is ideal. If the paving is
already in place, why not lift random slabs to vary the texture?

Do weeded patios and paths result in too many unforgiving lines?
Why not plant up the cracks? If there's enough soil beneath
the slabs and the climate is generally kind, try the houseplant
mind-your-own-business with its appealing, rambling habit.
To survive hot weather, look for drought-proof plants such as
woolly thyme, or self-seeding plants suitable for the conditions.
If you are short of soil, the humble moss may be enough
to soften the area.

If you are creating a path through the garden, try to make it wide
enough for a wheel-barrow – or you could spend years ploughing into
borders as you clear debris from other beds.

If you're installing a hot tub, surround it with decking or
paving rather than gravel or you could find that the tub seats quickly
become peppered with stones.

Lawns

**Achieving a perfectly smooth expanse of immaculate,
emerald green lawn remains for most of us a distant dream,
as our plots and ambitions are constantly thwarted by one
or more of the three principal pests – weeds, animals and
children. Don't despair, however, as there are some simple
measures that can help make your vision a reality.**

Treat mower blades with spray lubricant at the beginning
and end of the season. It improves the cutting action and makes
cleaning a breeze.

Does your lawn suffer from moss invasion? Don't just reach for the
box of chemicals. Upright mosses indicate acid soil that could benefit
from a dose of lime. Trailing mosses flourish where there's poor
drainage and that might be solved if you give overhanging branches a
haircut. Some forms are even encouraged when you cut lawns too
closely. Identify the cause and you'll save money and time.

Did you know that a weed can produce as many as
250,000 seeds a year? It makes sense, therefore, to mow before
the weed heads bear fruit, so you can stop a whole new generation
of weeds from taking root in the lawn.

To help control moss, reduce disease, strengthen growth and
give the lawn a lovely bright colour, apply lawn sand, which contains
iron sulphate.

When you are sowing a new lawn, be sure to use seed that is
guaranteed weed-free, or years of frustrating labour will take root
alongside the new grass.

Light rain provides the perfect conditions for using lawn
feed as it prevents scorching.

Try to avoid using nitrogen fertilizer as autumn approaches.
It can make the growth soft and disease prone.

It's difficult to predict when the last lawn cut will take place.
If it's too close to the first frost, then it could spell disaster for the
grass. So don't forget to raise the cutting height of the mower blades
at the end of summer to prevent subsequent lawn damage.

Worms are the gardener's friend – they help to break
down organic material and aerate the soil – so simply brush unsightly
worm casts off the lawn with a besom rather than kill the worms.

If you loathe your lawn for all the hard work and heartache
it gives you, why not turn it into a wild-flower meadow? You don't
even have to grub up the existing grass – simply introduce seeds or
install plug plants from reputable domestic suppliers to the existing
grass. Aim for about 85 per cent grasses and 15 per cent wild
flowers – avoiding rampant ryegrass. For spring flowering,
choose primroses, cowslips and yellow rattle, and for summer
go for harebells, common knapweed and field scabious. Then all
you have to do is mow once a year after flowering to
keep the grasses in check.

Green Gardens

We now know that excessive use of man-made substances is harming the world we live in. As we reject the quick-fix solutions that rely on harmful chemical aids, it's time to turn again to the commonsense ground rules that generations of past gardeners relied upon.

The lifeblood of a garden is compost, and fortunately it's easy to make your own. There are no hard-and-fast rules, but it is advisable to site your heap, bin, wire-mesh container, open-topped wooden box or tumbler in a distant corner of the garden. To make rich, nutritious compost, you can use any number of vegetable items, which will heat up together and rot down to a dry, crumbly, rich brown medium. Other popular ingredients include grass cuttings, weeds (without seed heads), peelings, pet bedding and leaves. The most dedicated add nail clippings, hair and even urine. Don't add meat scraps or four-legged scavengers will take an interest. Experts say it's best to layer items, but even if you don't you will in time produce nutritious compost for little or no cost.

A day spent choosing seeds in the garden centre
in the depths of winter can be a wonderful tonic. But for free seeds,
try collecting them from your own garden. The time to harvest
is when the flower head is dead and drying. Store the seed in
food bags or clean margarine tubs, not forgetting to label them and
then treat as you would commercially bought seeds.

Spread the ashes from a wood fire or bonfire around plant bases –
they are rich in potash and double as a slug deterrent.
But don't use ash from a coal fire as it will kill off plants. It's best
saved for the foundations of paths or patios.

Scrub and save wooden lolly sticks to use as plant markers. An old
venetian blind can also be chopped up to provide useful tags.

Don't toss away tin buckets, cans, old baths, plastic tubs or
saucepans. With luck, they'll already have a lived-in look and, laden
with blooms, will be full of cottage-garden charm. One enterprising
publican turned an abandoned Ford Fiesta into a planter/talking point.
Remember to drill drainage holes where necessary.

Take pride in being a 'second-hand Rose' and reap benefits in the
bank as well as the garden. Garage and car-boot sales often yield
cheap garden tools in sound condition. You should avoid electrical
items though, as faulty products could pose a potential hazard.
You can also scoop up statuary, bird baths or troughs at
architectural salvagers or antiques fairs.

Peat bogs are an over-plundered resource, and gardeners are the main target customers. You should, therefore, avoid buying peat, or compost containing peat, especially as experts say it can be satisfactorily replaced by a number of products, including coir. It may cost a little more in the short term, but in the long term it will help to cut the cost of the environmental damage to the landscape and wildlife which inhabit the bogs.

Protect tender, newly planted seedlings with a plastic collar cut from the body of an empty plastic lemonade bottle. It acts as a draught excluder and a slug and snail fence. You can cut at least three collars from every 2-litre bottle.

Put spare guttering to good use inside the greenhouse by suspending it to provide an aerial plant holder. It is slim and sleek, easy to water and makes welcome extra space at busy times.

Economize on the use of water around the garden by
installing a water butt that will conserve rainwater for dry days.
Liberal mulching around thirsty plants will also save a can or two
and help keep the nation's water table healthy at the same time.

After hard-boiling eggs, cool the pan water and use it on thirsty
plants – it's full of minerals from the eggshells. The cooled
water from boiled vegetables and the fish tank is also a bonus for
plants in containers.

Use old tights as ties around the garden. They are perfect for securing the fleshy stems of tomato plants.

If you get a fragile parcel through the post, don't ditch the wadding. Bubble wrap can protect pots and the plant roots in them from frost.

Use discarded supermarket orange and lemon nets to store bulbs, dried onions and even garlic. Thread string around the ripped opening to draw the ends together and then hang on a hook.

Wildlife Gardens

Watching wild animals and birds flitting about the garden can be at least as pleasurable as seeing young plants flourish and bloom. And it's a compliment – a sign that an ecosystem is at work – when wildlife is at home in your garden. Here are some tips on how to embrace nature.

Don't prune or move shrubs and hedges at nesting time. You'll be depriving birds of a home in which to raise their young. Put off the job until late summer when the fledglings have flown.

Insects are nature's pollinators and every garden needs a broad spectrum of our six-legged friends to thrive and survive. Keep bees, wasps, butterflies, hoverflies, moths and ladybirds happy by planting corn marigolds, pot marigolds, broad beans, borage, buddleia, night-scented stocks, nasturtiums, the poached egg plant, Californian poppies, sunflowers and sedum. Make sure you water them during droughts or nectar production will grind to a halt.

Simplicity is key in the wildlife garden, especially in the choice of flowers. Double-flowering varieties look exotic and extravagant but they are bad news for insects, who struggle to penetrate the more complex flower heads. Stick to single-flowering types at least some of the time.

Include a wild area in your garden so nature can provide for itself. Nettles, for example, are a vital food source for the caterpillars of native butterflies, but are largely eliminated from tended gardens.

If you use a chemical spray for pest control, apply to blighted plants at night to minimize the risk to pollinating or predator insects, which won't be around in such numbers as in the day.

For short spells in the spring and summer, it is helpful to
keep birds off seedlings and crops. Try making your own low-impact
bird scarer using ribbon or tinsel on sticks. You can also tie tin cans
closely together on a piece of string so they crash together in a
breeze. Or put up bells, kites or even make your own scarecrow.
Remember to take down the device as soon as the crop is harvested
or you risk the birds becoming familiar with and contemptuous of it.
Alternatively, stake out a seeded area with twigs and then wind wool,
cotton or string between them to make a homespun net.

Consider putting up wildlife lodges in your garden to give
animals and beneficial insects the best chance of happy life.
Lodges are available for ladybirds, lacewings, bumble bees, bats,
hedgehogs, dormice, fieldmice and birds ranging in size
from tits to owls. There are also butterfly feeders – just add
sugar water – and boxes with an integral spy system that offer an
inside view on the resident's activities.

Keep bird baths topped up during dry spells. And moisten crusts
before adding them to the bird table to help keep birds hydrated.

When installing a bird table, enclose its supporting post inside
a piece of plastic drainpipe about 76cm (30in) long so that predatory
cats can't easily climb up it. If you are making your
own bird table, another simple deterrent is a small circular platform
placed just below the one intended for feathered visitors.

You can fill a new pond with tap water if you leave it for
two weeks before adding foliage or fish. Ideally, a new pond should
have a couple of bucketfuls of water taken from an existing pond to
get the benefit of valuable micro-organisms that will give it a
natural head start.

Any food left in the pond five minutes after feeding time should be removed with a net. Uneaten food will rot, pollute the water and put fish stocks at risk.

Beware the sleeping hedgehog during autumn clean-ups. It is likely to hide away in bonfire piles and might lurk under leaves that you approach with the sharp and potentially lethal prongs of a fork.

Leave flower heads on teasels and sunflowers at the end of the growing season. They are not only hauntingly beautiful but provide a valuable food source for birds.

Gardening Glossary

Garden-speak sometimes sounds like a different language. Use this basic guide to get a new insight into gardening techniques.

Annuals Plants that die off after their growing season and have to be replaced.

Biological controls The introduction of living things, including nematodes, predatory midges and parasitic wasps, to control or eliminate garden pests.

Biennials Plants that complete their life cycle in two years.

Bulbs Perennial plants that have an underground food storage system.

Chitting Laying seed potatoes budding side up in an egg box or seed tray without soil, and leaving in a warm light place until they have sprouted roots.

Cloche Transparent plant protector made of glass, plastic or fleece.

Companion planting Putting different plants side by side to assist in organic pest control.

Cordons Single-stemmed trees trained along a wall, trellis or knee-high fence.

Cuttings Making new plants from old by taking a section of stem, root or leaf and placing it in soil or water until it grows its own root system.

Double digging Digging to the equivalent depth of two spade blades.

Earthing up Loosely covering new shoots with compost in early spring to protect them from the cold.

Layering Method of plant propagation in which the stem is stripped of leaves and pinned into soil. When it develops a root system it can be severed from the parent plant.

Mulch Cover for soil.

Nitrogen Essential element of plant food that prompts healthy growth.

Pergola A framework of wooden beams providing a sheltered walkway or seating area.

Perennials Long lasting plants with flexible root stems that die down in winter and grow again each year from hardy roots.

Phosphate A fertiliser with phosphorus that helps fruiting and root formation.

Potager A decorative veggie patch dating from Tudor times.

Potash A fertiliser containing potassium, which helps plants use sunlight for growth.

Scarifying Removing moss and debris from the lawn by rake or powered scarifier.

Take Five for...

*The following lists of 5 plants
are grouped to give you a few ideas
of the varieties which are suitable
for different locations and types
of soil. So, whether you want to
create a bold, brightly coloured
border, a pleasantly perfumed
patch or simply an eye catching
window box or container display,
these top tips will help to ease
the indecision at the garden
centre or when buying on the
internet and start you on your
way to green-fingered glory.*

A Tropical Border

Canna 'Durban'

Lobelia 'Tupa'

Dahlia 'Bishop of Llandaff'

Kniphofia Caulescens 'Red
Hot Poker'

Ricinus Communis 'Castor
Oil Plant'

An Acid Soil

Azaleas

Rhododendrons

Camellias

Ericas

Pieris

A Clay Soil

Acer plantanoides

Amelanchier lamarckii
(snowy mespilus)

Ribes sanguineum
(flowering currant)

Roses – most varieties
but check the label

Philadelphus

Annuals

Alyssum
Antirrhinum
Delphinium
Impatiens
Verbena

A Shady Spot

Hostas
Hellebores
Lilies of the Valley
Impatiens
Evergreen ivy

A Scented Garden

Tobacco plant (white)
Honeysuckle
Jasmine
Sweet peas
Lonicera

A Container Garden
Camellias

Abutilon

Cordyline

Cistus

Lavender

Alpines
Aubretia

Gentiana

Oxalis

Saxifraga

Silene

Trailing plants for Window Boxes
Chlorophytum (Spider plant)

Trailing Fuchsias

Hedera (Ivy)

Nasturtiums

Lobelia

Flowering Shrubs
Fuchsias

Cornus (Dogwood)

Prunus

Rhododendron

Mahonia